A Gift for You

As a thank you for investing in your faith and this book, we want to gift you with this beautiful, complimentary *Fear Less* bonus pack.

Download Your FREE Bonus Pack

at www.theholymess.com/fearless

This free digital bonus includes:

- Printable 30 day reading plan.

- Exclusive behind-the-scenes interview with the author.

- Phone wallpapers

- Printable Bible verse note cards.

Go to <u>www.theholymess.com/fearless</u> or scan the QR code below with your smart phone to download yours now.

Fear

LESS

30 DEVOTIONS FOR COURAGEOUS FAITH

BY SARA BORGSTEDE

This book is dedicated to every person who battles depression, anxiety, and panic. You are **incredibly brave**, and you are not alone.

Table of Contents

Introduction

Strengthen your faith in just seven minutes!

Are you worried?

There's plenty to be anxious about in today's world.

At the time that this devotion series was written, the coronavirus was new. Fear ran rampant in our country and throughout the world.

Schools closed. Businesses closed. People were required to wear masks in public. Each day there were news broadcasts about more people becoming infected, government officials argued over policies, and new guidelines were being established.

God tells us in the Bible to "fear not." (In fact, it's in the Bible over 300 times!) How is this possible with so much happening that is frightening and overwhelming?

As Christians, we are called to face our fears. God tells us that He is in control. He has plans for each of us and for our world.

Having faith that is bigger than fear isn't easy.

Yet with God's help, it's possible.

Join me for the next thirty days as we learn what the Bible says about how to trust God during any challenging circumstances you are currently facing.

Let's journey together.

How to Use Seven-Minute Devotions

In this fast-paced world, carving out time for prayer and Bible study is tough. You want to focus on growing in faith, but it's not easy with so many other commitments.

These devotions are meant to be completed in just seven minutes a day, making them doable for someone with even the busiest schedule.

Here's how seven-minute devotions work:

- Read the day's Bible passage – *three minutes.*

- Read the devotion – *two minutes.*

- Think about or write answers to the reflection question, such as in a journal or notebook – *two minutes.*

(Optional) If you have more time, watch each day's video or spend time in prayer.

May God bless your efforts.

Day 1: Are You Guarding Your Heart with God's Peace?

Bible passage:

Rejoice in the Lord always; again I will say, rejoice. Let your reasonableness be known to everyone. The Lord is at hand; do not be anxious about anything, but in everything by prayer and supplication with thanksgiving let your requests be made known to God. And the peace of God, which surpasses all understanding, will guard your hearts and your minds in Christ Jesus.

Philippians 4:4-7

As a Christian, it is important to guard your heart. Proverbs 4:23 says, "Above all else, guard your heart, for it is the wellspring of life."

How can you protect your heart?

One place where you need to continually guard your heart is with social media. I love scrolling through Facebook and Instagram to keep up with friends and interact with people who visit my website, The Holy Mess. Yet I must continually remind myself that I'm looking at other people's highlight reels, not their real lives.

Another place where it's important to guard your heart is with national and international news. The goal of news outlets is to make money, not consider your mental health and wellbeing. Yes, it's good to know what's going on in the world, but take care that you aren't over consuming the information they are selling.

Finally, it's important to guard your heart from your own thoughts and emotions. I like to say guarding your thoughts is like keeping track of a room full of two-year-olds. Without supervision, things are fun for a while but soon enough someone is going to get hurt.

Today's passage from Philippians reminds you that the way to guard your heart is with God's peace that passes all understanding. We tend to think of peace as passive, but this verse tells us that God's peace is active. How amazing that peace can guard your heart! Slow down and allow God's peace to rule your life.

Reflection question: How can you allow God's peace to guard your heart today?

Day 1 devotion video: https://youtu.be/cbPA1FrZvCY

Scan the QR code below to watch.

Day 2: How Can You Trust in the Lord with ALL Your Heart?

Bible passage:

Trust in the Lord with all your heart,
    and do not lean on your own understanding.
In all your ways acknowledge him,
    and he will make straight your paths.
Be not wise in your own eyes;
    fear the Lord, and turn away from evil.
It will be healing to your flesh
    and refreshment to your bones.

Proverbs 3:5-8

This passage of Scripture is one of the most famous in the Bible and with good reason. Isn't it true that you need the continual reminder to trust in God? I sure do. He will give you the straight path to take.

Yet, what does it look like to trust God with all your heart? It isn't easy. If you are like me, you trust what you see. You trust things you've tried and with which you are familiar. You trust the advice of friends or mentors. Trusting a God you cannot see is difficult.

This passage reminds you not to trust your own understanding. In today's world, you have an abundance of information. A quick Google search will guide you to almost anything you want to know.

But is it trustworthy? Your source of information might or not be worthy of your trust, but this verse tells you to put your faith in God above all else. Today, focus on God and His Word as your source of truth.

Reflection question: How can you put your trust in God for decisions you are facing?

Day 2 devotion video: https://youtu.be/0eiKlatrI7M

Day 3: Did You Know You Have the Power of God Inside You?

Bible passage:

God is our refuge and strength,
    a very present help in trouble.
Therefore we will not fear though the earth gives way,
    though the mountains be moved into the heart of
the sea,
though its waters roar and foam,
    though the mountains tremble at its swelling.

There is a river whose streams make glad the city of
God,
    the holy habitation of the Most High.
God is in the midst of her; she shall not be moved;
    God will help her when morning dawns.
The nations rage, the kingdoms totter;
    he utters his voice, the earth melts.

Psalm 46:1-6

You know what is incredibly amazing? The God who created mountains, oceans, waterfalls, and forests, is the same God who lives inside of you.

Our family lives in Western New York, and we are fortunate to live just a short drive away from Niagara Falls. We've been there to visit many times. Each time I go, I am once again in awe of the powerful force of the water. Seeing the majestic waterfalls is beautiful, exciting, and yes, even a little bit scary.

The next time you are overwhelmed or afraid, remember that the God who created all these wonders is the same God you have at work in your life. There's nothing you need to fear and absolutely nothing you cannot overcome.

Reflection question: What's an area of your life where you need the power of the God of the universe to work?

Day 3 devotion video: https://youtu.be/0IyMw6mfu1U

Day 4: What Does It Mean to Be Still?

Bible passage:

The Lord of hosts is with us;
    the God of Jacob is our fortress.

Come, behold the works of the Lord,
    how he has brought desolations on the earth.
He makes wars cease to the end of the earth;
    he breaks the bow and shatters the spear;
    he burns the chariots with fire.
"Be still, and know that I am God.
    I will be exalted among the nations,
    I will be exalted in the earth!"

Psalm 46:7-10

I'm not so great at stillness.

I like being busy and always have different projects and plans going.

As I write this devotion, we are currently on stay-at-home restrictions due to COVID-19, and it has been a big change. While my life is still busy with kids to school from home and a husband working in the house, it has still been a time of more rest. We aren't driving places, running around to kids' activities, going to church, or going to the gym.

This has been a time for me to evaluate what it means to be still. Some of the blessings have been more time with my family, daily devotions at breakfast, eating meals together, and simply time to relax.

Once I return to regular activities, it will be important to evaluate ways I can continue to be still in the middle of a busy life.

Do you struggle with an overly busy schedule? How can you find stillness?

Reflection question: In what ways do you need to slow down life's pace so that you can be still before God?

Day 4 devotion video: https://youtu.be/q0ZCWFD1_Fl

Day 5: Do You Delight in Your Weaknesses?

Bible reading:

So to keep me from becoming conceited because of the surpassing greatness of the revelations, a thorn was given me in the flesh, a messenger of Satan to harass me, to keep me from becoming conceited. Three times I pleaded with the Lord about this, that it should leave me. But he said to me, "My grace is sufficient for you, for my power is made perfect in weakness." Therefore I will boast all the more gladly of my weaknesses, so that the power of Christ may rest upon me. For the sake of Christ, then, I am content with weaknesses, insults, hardships, persecutions, and calamities. For when I am weak, then I am strong.

2 Corinthians 12:7-10

I have a hard time with the concept of delighting in my weaknesses. I want my weaknesses to be gone, and I want them gone yesterday. Forget delighting in weakness. I don't even want it to exist.

One of my biggest life struggles is with food and my weight. For the last fifteen years, I've been maintaining a weight loss of over one-hundred pounds. While God has brought me so much healing in this area, it's still a daily challenge. After years of binge eating and compulsively overeating, I've come a long way, but the temptation to overeat or binge is still there.

I have prayed often for God to remove this thorn from my flesh. So far, His answer has been no.

Yet, I also see, just like Paul in this passage, how God is growing my faith in this area. I am continually humbled. I continue to turn to Him for help in times of temptation. I see that God is strong where I am weak.

I haven't given up on praying for God to take this issue from me. Whether He does or doesn't, I'll lean on Him for guidance.

Reflection question: Do you have a "thorn in the flesh" issue that hasn't gone away? Turn to God for help with it today.

Day 5 devotion video: https://youtu.be/ClMoc967sxU

Day 6: You Have the Power!

Bible passage:

For God gave us a spirit not of fear but of power and love and self-control.

2 Timothy 1:7

Do you feel powerful? Often the last thing I feel is powerful. I feel weak, weary, or overwhelmed.

Yet, this passage says you are amazingly powerful. This power does not come from inside of you. It doesn't come from how good you are, the tasks you accomplish, your family or connections, where you live, or what type of car you drive. Your power comes from the Holy Spirit at work inside of you.

The Bible passage goes on to say that you have love. You have God's love, which means you have the ability to love those in your life who aren't very lovable.

You have self-discipline. This self-discipline isn't about willpower or relying on grit to accomplish important tasks. Self-control is a fruit of the spirit and fruits of the spirit are gifts of faith.

How will you use the gifts of power, love, and self-control today?

Reflection question: Think of an area in your life where you feel weak or powerless. How can you use God's power to grow stronger?

Day 6 devotion video: https://youtu.be/SD0dspYyz7Y

Day 7: How to Stop Anxiety in Its Tracks

Bible passage:

But now thus says the Lord,
he who created you, O Jacob,
    he who formed you, O Israel:
"Fear not, for I have redeemed you;
    I have called you by name, you are mine.
When you pass through the waters, I will be with you;
    and through the rivers, they shall not overwhelm
you;
when you walk through fire you shall not be burned,
    and the flame shall not consume you.
For I am the Lord your God,
    the Holy One of Israel, your Savior.
I give Egypt as your ransom,
    Cush and Seba in exchange for you.
Because you are precious in my eyes,
    and honored, and I love you,
I give men in return for you,
    peoples in exchange for your life.
Fear not, for I am with you;
    I will bring your offspring from the east,
    and from the west I will gather you.
I will say to the north, Give up,
    and to the south, Do not withhold;
bring my sons from afar
    and my daughters from the end of the earth,
everyone who is called by my name,
    whom I created for my glory,
    whom I formed and made."

Isaiah 43:1-7

One of our teenage sons is adopted from foster care, and he suffered trauma and abuse before he came to live with us.

All of his life he has struggled with extremely challenging behavior, but things came to a head during the years when he was ten to twelve years old. Our family barely survived as we endured one crisis after another due to his violence and aggression. Every wall of our home had holes punched in it. We called the police so often that we were told to quit calling.

Our marriage, our finances, our mental health, and our other children suffered greatly. Finally, after years of advocacy, our son entered residential treatment and lived away from our family for an extended period of time.

Today, as I write these words our son is about to celebrate his sixteenth birthday. He is back living with our family and is thriving. He goes to school. He has friends, goes to church, and takes Tae Kwon Do and piano lessons. Sure, we still have our issues, but in many ways he's a typical teenager.

When we were in the midst of our toughest challenges with our son, one day I sat on a ragged couch in our therapist's office and poured out my heart about my extreme anxiety and fears for his future. Instead of telling me not to worry so much, she suggested the opposite.

The therapist told me to go ahead and think about the worst-case scenario. What if my son killed himself? What if he hurt someone else? What if he went to jail? She was honest that those things might happen, and I needed to prepare myself for that reality.

Rather than overwhelming me, her words brought me a certain comfort as I pondered the fact that yes, each of these scenarios would be incredibly painful, but I also had faith that God would bring me through it. Sometimes the key to anxiety is to face the worst-case scenario head on and remember that God's grace will see you through.

Reflection question: Is there a worst-case scenario you need to face head on to stop your anxious thoughts? If it happens, how will you lean on God for help?

Day 7 devotion video: https://youtu.be/wW-HbPRkGFU

Day 8: Have You Ever Been Falsely Accused?

Bible passage:

Be gracious to me, O God, for man tramples on me;
    all day long an attacker oppresses me;
my enemies trample on me all day long,
    for many attack me proudly.
When I am afraid,
    I put my trust in you.
In God, whose word I praise,
    in God I trust; I shall not be afraid.
    What can flesh do to me?

Psalm 56:1-4

Have you ever been wrongly accused of something you didn't do wrong? Maybe it's an ex-spouse who says untrue things about you in court or a co-worker who blames you for something you didn't do. Perhaps a family member blames you for the problems in a relationship.

Most of us have been falsely accused at one time or another.

One of the most painful experiences of my life was when my husband and I were accused and taken to court for a crime we didn't commit. We lived through many painful months of waiting, sleepless nights, and expensive attorney fees that were well beyond our budget. Thankfully, our story eventually had a happy ending.

When you are falsely accused, it's easy to let bitterness take root.

This passage from Psalms encourages you to trust in God as your source of strength and comfort. This isn't easy when you are in the middle of false accusations! Yet God's Word challenges you to trust Him above all. Focus on God instead of worrying about what other people think, say, or do.

Reflection question: Have you been falsely accused of something you didn't do wrong? Have you put your trust in God to handle it? Say a prayer to let go of bitterness over the situation.

Day 8 devotion video: https://youtu.be/qVfQRkvPNKo

Day 9: When Life Throws You a Curve Ball

Bible passage:

Humble yourselves, therefore, under the mighty hand of God so that at the proper time he may exalt you, casting all your anxieties on him, because he cares for you. Be sober-minded; be watchful. Your adversary the devil prowls around like a roaring lion, seeking someone to devour. Resist him, firm in your faith, knowing that the same kinds of suffering are being experienced by your brotherhood throughout the world. And after you have suffered a little while, the God of all grace, who has called you to his eternal glory in Christ, will himself restore, confirm, strengthen, and establish you. To him be the dominion forever and ever. Amen.

1 Peter 5:6-11

All of us have experienced times when life throws us a curve ball. Plans change. Problems happen. Priorities must be rearranged.

During these times, the situation is not usually your fault. Something happened that was outside your control.

However, as much as these circumstances are out of your control, giving in to sinful behaviors within the situation is not okay. You may be tempted to snap at loved ones, engage in addictive behaviors, or wallow in anxiety.

Today's Bible passage from 1 Peter talks about how our enemy is like a roaring lion looking for someone to devour. This is especially true in times of crisis, when the devil works overtime to pull you away from God.

You have a power that is stronger than any attack of the enemy. James 4:7 says to resist the devil and he will flee. At the name of Jesus he has to be gone! This is both a relief and a challenge. If you are in the middle of a tough life circumstance, don't use it as an excuse to give in to the devil's temptations. Resist, and he will flee.

Reflection question: Have you been tempted to give in to sinful behaviors during a time of crisis? How can you resist the devil during these times?

Day 9 devotion video: https://youtu.be/L8LkDkSPbvA

Day 10: Consider the Lilies

Bible passage:

"Therefore I tell you, do not be anxious about your life, what you will eat or what you will drink, nor about your body, what you will put on. Is not life more than food, and the body more than clothing? Look at the birds of the air: they neither sow nor reap nor gather into barns, and yet your heavenly Father feeds them. Are you not of more value than they? And which of you by being anxious can add a single hour to his span of life? And why are you anxious about clothing? Consider the lilies of the field, how they grow: they neither toil nor spin, yet I tell you, even Solomon in all his glory was not arrayed like one of these. But if God so clothes the grass of the field, which today is alive and tomorrow is thrown into the oven, will he not much more clothe you, O you of little faith? Therefore do not be anxious, saying, 'What shall we eat?' or 'What shall we drink?' or 'What shall we wear?' For the Gentiles seek after all these things, and your heavenly Father knows that you need them all. But seek first the kingdom of God and his righteousness, and all these things will be added to you.

Therefore do not be anxious about tomorrow, for tomorrow will be anxious for itself. Sufficient for the day is its own trouble."

Matthew 6:25-34

The sixth chapter of Matthew includes one of the most beautiful passages in all of Scripture where Jesus, as part of the Sermon on the Mount, encourages us to consider the lilies, the grass, and the birds of the air.

None of these does anything to take care of themselves, yet God lovingly tends each one. How much more God loves you as one of his people!

Through this passage, and all of the Bible, Jesus tells you not to worry. This is both a comfort and a challenge. It's easy to slip into anxious thoughts and challenging to take those thoughts captive to obey Christ, yet this is your calling as a Christian. Do not worry. Instead, take your anxious thoughts to God who cares for you.

Reflection question: What are you worried about today? Ask God to take care of this worry for you.

Day 10 devotion video: https://youtu.be/e_u-uSZ_dLo

Day 11: Friend, Lift Up Your Eyes!

Bible passage:

I lift up my eyes to the hills.
    From where does my help come?
My help comes from the Lord,
    who made heaven and earth.

He will not let your foot be moved;
    he who keeps you will not slumber.
Behold, he who keeps Israel
    will neither slumber nor sleep.

The Lord is your keeper;
    the Lord is your shade on your right hand.
The sun shall not strike you by day,
    nor the moon by night.

The Lord will keep you from all evil;
    he will keep your life.
The Lord will keep
    your going out and your coming in
    from this time forth and forevermore.

Psalm 121

Psalm 121 has always had special meaning for me because it was the theme verse for a trip to the Holy Land I took while I was in college. Believe it or not, my husband proposed to me on that trip. A few years later, we had this verse read at our wedding, and we both hold it as extra meaningful for our marriage.

An important part of this psalm is in verse three where it says God will not let your foot slip. For years before I was able to lose one-hundred pounds and keep it off, I felt like I was constantly starting over with my weight loss. I thought I had failed. I told myself I was "back to square one" and "getting back on the wagon" to attempt to lose the weight again.

When I started therapy for my eating issues, my therapist shared an important new way for me to think of my weight loss journey. Every time I start again, I'm not starting from the beginning because I have experience. I'm smarter and stronger now.

Think of it like climbing a mountain. When you fall down, you just fall down right where you are. You get up, brush yourself off and get going again. You don't slide all the way to the bottom if you slip.

Whatever situations you are facing today, remember that even if you fail in the moment, you are not starting over at the beginning. Focus on getting back up and trying again.

Reflection question: What situation are you struggling with today where it will help you to remember that you are not starting over?

Day 11 devotion video: https://youtu.be/9oOBaQEvKIU

Day 12: God Intends This for Your Good

Bible passage:

As for you, you meant evil against me, but God meant it for good, to bring it about that many people should be kept alive, as they are today.

Genesis 50:20

Today's reading is from a conversation Joseph had with his family. Joseph went through major life trauma. His family sold him into slavery. He was wrongly accused and thrown into jail. Yet God also continued to bless him, and he rose into power and saved his country from famine. Speaking to those same family members who sold him as a slave, Joseph tells them, "What you intended for harm, God intended for good."

Whatever challenges you are facing today, you can trust that God will bring good from them. You can trust that God will somehow work the details of your life for ultimate good.

Reflection question: What is a situation where you have seen God work good from a difficult time? Think of a current struggle you face. Consider how you can trust that God will somehow use it for good.

Day 12 devotion video: https://youtu.be/XnLrPx-COTs

Day 13: How's Your Mental Flexibility?

Bible passage:

Jesus Christ is the same yesterday and today and forever.

Hebrews 13:8

Have you heard of the concept of mental flexibility? This is the ability to shift your thought or course of action depending on the situation. Some of us are much better at mental flexibility than others. If you need a strict schedule that is always the same, you might struggle when things don't go your way. Some people with special needs especially struggle with being mentally flexible.

As a Christian, you can develop more mental flexibility because you trust that God is in control. Just like a tree with strong roots, your foundation in Christ is solid. Like the branches of a strong tree, you can bend and sway without breaking.

Reflection question: Are you mentally flexible? In what ways can you improve your mental flexibility?

Day 13 devotion video: https://youtu.be/o0AFEOs2KIs

Day 14: You Are Known

Bible Passage:

O Lord, you have searched me and known me!
You know when I sit down and when I rise up;
    you discern my thoughts from afar.
You search out my path and my lying down
    and are acquainted with all my ways.
Even before a word is on my tongue,
    behold, O Lord, you know it altogether.
You hem me in, behind and before,
    and lay your hand upon me.

Psalm 139:1-5

One of your deepest needs as a human being is to be known and understood. When someone else "gets" what you say, there is a feeling of acceptance and relief that another person understands your perspective.

My second daughter, Kiersten, has always been fiercely independent. When she was ten years old, she started begging us to dye her hair blue. For years I said, "No way!" but she was relentless. Finally, when she was twelve, I said she could dye her hair after her church confirmation day. The afternoon after the worship service, she was up in the bathroom dying her hair (and my bathroom sink and quite a few of my towels) blue.

Kiersten has a need to express who she is with her hair color. How do you express who you are? Some people use outward means, some use words, and some use behavior. Every person longs to be deeply known and understood.

Today, rest in the fact that God knows and understands you best of all.

Reflection question: How do you express your personality and desires? What does it mean to you that God sees and knows you?

Day 14 devotion video: https://youtu.be/pwZ5B1ybVIU

Day 15: Go or Stay, God is There

Bible passage:

Such knowledge is too wonderful for me;
    it is high; I cannot attain it.
Where shall I go from your Spirit?
    Or where shall I flee from your presence?
If I ascend to heaven, you are there!
    If I make my bed in Sheol, you are there!
If I take the wings of the morning
    and dwell in the uttermost parts of the sea,
even there your hand shall lead me,
    and your right hand shall hold me.

Psalm 139:6-10

As I write these words, our government leaders are making decisions about when to lift restrictions as part of the coronavirus quarantine. People are faced with individual decisions, too. Should I go back to church or the gym? Should I wear a mask when I go grocery shopping? These are tough questions with no simple answers, but today's Bible passage brings reassurance. Whether you go out or stay in, God is there.

No matter where you go or what you do, God has gone before you. God is with you now. God will be there in your future.

Reflection question: In what area of life do you have questions or fears about where you should go or what you should do? Reflect on the fact that God is already there.

Day 15 devotion video: https://youtu.be/6VehtSjNB7c

Day 16: Are You Ready for Battle?

Bible passage:

Finally, be strong in the Lord and in the strength of his might. Put on the whole armor of God, that you may be able to stand against the schemes of the devil. For we do not wrestle against flesh and blood, but against the rulers, against the authorities, against the cosmic powers over this present darkness, against the spiritual forces of evil in the heavenly places. Therefore take up the whole armor of God, that you may be able to withstand in the evil day, and having done all, to stand firm. Stand therefore, having fastened on the belt of truth, and having put on the breastplate of righteousness, and, as shoes for your feet, having put on the readiness given by the gospel of peace. In all circumstances take up the shield of faith, with which you can extinguish all the flaming darts of the evil one; and take the helmet of salvation, and the sword of the Spirit, which is the word of God, praying at all times in the Spirit, with all prayer and supplication. To that end, keep alert with all perseverance, making supplication for all the saints.

Ephesians 6:10-18

You, my friend, are facing a battle today. You have a real enemy, Satan, who makes it his full time job to attempt to pull you away from God.

Each of us faces different temptations depending on our history and personality. Your temptations may be addictions like food or alcohol, or your addictions could be worry, anxiety, gossip, or judging others.

These issues might seem overwhelming, but you have the power to fight them! God has given you a full armor to withstand anything the devil throws at you. You have the helmet of salvation and the shield of faith. You have the sword of the spirit which is the Word of God.

Ready? Let's go fight!

Reflection question: What battles are you facing today? How will you use the full armor of God to defeat our spiritual enemy, Satan?

Day 16 devotion video - https://youtu.be/cl-fqBdvoJw

Day 17: How to Get New Mercies

Bible passage:

The steadfast love of the Lord never ceases;
    his mercies never come to an end;
they are new every morning;
    great is your faithfulness.
"The Lord is my portion," says my soul,
    "therefore I will hope in him."
The Lord is good to those who wait for him,
    to the soul who seeks him.
It is good that one should wait quietly
    for the salvation of the Lord.

Lamentations 3:22-26

For many years, I was a stay-at-home mom. In addition to our five children, we were foster parents to thirty-five other children, mostly medically fragile babies. While this was rewarding and meaningful work, it was also exhausting. During those years, I felt like a little one was always hanging on my body, calling for mama, crying, or needing something from me.

Evenings were especially tough because my husband, who is a pastor, would come home for a quick dinner then leave again for church meetings. Getting the kids fed, bathed and to bed by myself often felt like it was pushing me to the edge of my sanity.

At the time I was one hundred pounds heavier than I am today, and I often used food in the evenings to numb my feelings of overwhelm. I overate dinner, ate more while I was cleaning up the dishes, ate snack after snack in front of the TV, and binged on ice cream and cookies.

When I shared with a friend about my nighttime struggles, she reminded me that God promises us new mercies in the morning. Rather that ruminating over all the mistakes I made during the day or focusing on my exhaustion level, why not go to bed and get some rest, looking forward to new mercies waiting for me in the morning? This perspective shift made a world of difference in my evening attitude.

Reflection question: Do you struggle with evening anxiety, overeating, or overwhelm? How can you get some rest instead and focus on God's mercies that will be new in the morning?

Day 17 devotion video: https://youtu.be/w3-nvZnkt_0

Day 18: Calm Storm or Calm You?

Bible passage:

One day he (Jesus) got into a boat with his disciples, and he said to them, "Let us go across to the other side of the lake." So they set out, and as they sailed he fell asleep. And a windstorm came down on the lake, and they were filling with water and were in danger. And they went and woke him, saying, "Master, Master, we are perishing!" And he awoke and rebuked the wind and the raging waves, and they ceased, and there was a calm. He said to them, "Where is your faith?" And they were afraid, and they marveled, saying to one another, "Who then is this, that he commands even winds and water, and they obey him?"

Luke 8:22-25

In today's Bible passage, we see the amazing power of Jesus when he calms a storm as he and his disciples are on the Sea of Galilee.

Before we dive into the deeper aspects of this Bible lesson, let's highlight the fact that Jesus was napping. (I'm an early riser and take a nap almost every day. Hooray for guilt-free naps!)

In this passage, we see that Jesus had the power with just his voice to calm a raging storm. What storms are you facing in your life right now? It might be relationship struggles, financial burdens, addictions, or depression. Maybe it's ongoing health issues or a difficult work situation. No matter the storm you are facing, Jesus is there with you and has the power to calm it.

Yet, it's important to remember that while Jesus has the power to calm the storms of your life, he might choose not to do so. Calming the storm might not be part of God's plan for you today.

Sometimes Jesus calms the storm, but sometimes He calms you instead.

Reflection question: What storms of life are you currently facing? If Jesus isn't calming the storm, is it possible He wants to calm you instead?

Day 18 devotion video: https://youtu.be/ydRP_it5oME

Day 19: Trouble Sleeping? Read this.

Bible passage:

In peace I will both lie down and sleep;
  for you alone, O Lord, make me dwell in safety.

Psalm 4:8

Do you have trouble sleeping? Many people who struggle with depression, anxiety, or worries find themselves awake in the middle of the night. I've been there.

Insomnia is such a lonely feeling. In the quiet hours of the night, you feel like the whole world is asleep and you alone are awake, looking at the clock. You might be busy calculating how many hours of sleep you can get if you fall asleep immediately, then worrying even more when you still can't fall asleep.

Use this Bible passage as a reminder that you can lie down, rest, and sleep in peace because God is in control of your life. Instead of recalculating how many hours are left until the alarm goes off, spend the time with God in prayer. Don't worry about tomorrow because God will be there to meet your needs, whether you are facing the day tired or well-rested.

Reflection: Do you have trouble sleeping? How can you use this verse from Psalms for comfort?

Day 19 devotion video: - https://youtu.be/YFRg43I9YL8

Day 20: How to Have Faith to Walk on Water

Bible passage:

 Immediately he made the disciples get into the boat and go before him to the other side, while he dismissed the crowds. And after he had dismissed the crowds, he went up on the mountain by himself to pray. When evening came, he was there alone, but the boat by this time was a long way from the land, beaten by the waves, for the wind was against them. And in the fourth watch of the night he came to them, walking on the sea. But when the disciples saw him walking on the sea, they were terrified, and said, "It is a ghost!" and they cried out in fear. But immediately Jesus spoke to them, saying, "Take heart; it is I. Do not be afraid."

And Peter answered him, "Lord, if it is you, command me to come to you on the water." He said, "Come." So Peter got out of the boat and walked on the water and came to Jesus. But when he saw the wind, he was afraid, and beginning to sink he cried out, "Lord, save me." Jesus immediately reached out his hand and took hold of him, saying to him, "O you of little faith, why did you doubt?" And when they got into the boat, the wind ceased. And those in the boat worshipped him, saying, "Truly you are the Son of God."

Matthew 14:22-33

Today's Bible reading of Jesus walking on water and Peter coming out to meet him is one of my favorite passages of Scripture. Peter joins Jesus in walking on water but sinks when he sees the wind and waves.

Jesus asks Peter why his faith is lacking and grabs him to safety.

Here are three important truths to take away from this passage.

1.Get out of the boat.

2.Focus on Jesus.

3.If you fall, Jesus will catch you.

First, get out of the boat! You can't walk in faith if you are staying fearfully in the boat. I feel like Peter often gets a bad rap when we study this passage. Maybe his faith was weak, but hey, at least he had faith enough to get out of the boat and meet Jesus! Yet, Jesus rebukes him, so you may feel confusing about Jesus' words.

One of my Tae Kwon Do teachers once told me (on a day in class when I was getting an endless stream of corrections) that a teacher who is hard on you, believes in you. Corrections help you grow.

Second, focus on Jesus. Peter only started to sink when he looked at his circumstances and became afraid. Don't look around. Look to Jesus.

Finally, remember that Jesus will catch you when you fall. We don't know exactly what this looked like, but Peter doesn't seem to have even reached out for help. Jesus just grabs him up and takes him back to safety. Sometimes, it's scary to step out in faith, but remember that Jesus will be there to catch you.

Reflection question: In what area of life do you need to step out of the boat?

Day 20 devotion video: https://youtu.be/hrRrsuwtVME

Day 21: What is Courage? (And How Can I Get Some?)

Bible passage:

Have I not commanded you? Be strong and courageous. Do not be frightened, and do not be dismayed, for the Lord your God is with you wherever you go."

Joshua 1:9

Today's Bible passage tells you to be strong and courageous because God is with you wherever you go.

Often, I don't feel courageous. I feel scared, anxious, or overwhelmed. How does courage happen?

I love blogger, writer, and speaker Ruth Soukup's definition of courage, which is, "Courage is not the absence of fear. Courage is feeling fear and doing it anyway." You might think you need courage to act, but most often the opposite is true. You need to act to find your courage.

As a Christian, you don't muster up courage from inside of yourself. Courage comes from trusting that God lives inside of you and is giving you the strength to step out in faith.

Reflection question: In what area of life do you need to take steps of faith, trusting that the courage will come from action?

Day 21 devotion video: https://youtu.be/uT3z650sgW4

Day 22: You Can't Mess This Up

Bible passage:

I know that you can do all things,
    and that no purpose of yours can be thwarted.
'Who is this that hides counsel without knowledge?'
Therefore I have uttered what I did not understand,
    things too wonderful for me, which I did not know.

Job 42:2-3

God's plans cannot be thwarted. That means that no matter what, what God has planned will happen. I find this to be a tremendous relief because I mess things up all the time! I fall back into old sinful habits. I open my mouth and quickly insert my foot by saying the wrong thing. I make decisions and then later wish I hadn't made them.

Yet, through all this, God's plans prevail.

My husband, Mike, is a pastor. After we had served in ministry at our church in Indiana for several years, Mike received a call to serve at a church in Colorado. We faced a difficult decision. We felt called to continue our ministry in Indiana, yet we also felt called to ministry in Colorado.

Mike asked a mentor for advice. Which church should we choose? Mike's mentor wisely encouraged him that no matter what decision he made, God would work it for good. This was a relief. We ended up taking the call to Colorado and served there for sixteen years. We had many wonderful experiences in Colorado, both in ministry and as a family.

Reflection question: Are you facing a decision or challenging life situation where you wonder what God's plans are for you? Rest assured that no matter what you decide, you can't mess up God's ultimate purpose for you and your life.

Day 22 devotion video: https://youtu.be/6_gy6S9ezb8

Day 23: This Will Change Your Life

Bible passage:

We destroy arguments and every lofty opinion raised against the knowledge of God, and take every thought captive to obey Christ.

2 Corinthians 10:5

A life-changing Biblical concept is learning to take your thoughts captive to obey Christ, based on 2 Corinthians 10:5. For much of my life, I didn't understand that I could change my thoughts. I figured my thoughts were just my thoughts. I went about living my life dealing with whatever came into my head.

Yet, this verse is clear that part of my work of spiritual maturity is to change my thoughts. Think of it like this. Your thoughts are like a room full of unsupervised two-year-olds. Sure, it's fun for a while, but soon enough someone is going to get hurt. Left unattended, your thoughts run you into all types of crazy places.

Here's a three-step process to take your thoughts captive to obey Christ.

1. Recognize your thoughts.

2. Question your thoughts.

3. Use Scripture to guide your thoughts into the Truth.

First, recognize your thoughts. You might go through life simply thinking things or saying phrases to yourself without question. Where does your thought life take you? Start to pay attention.

Second, question if your thoughts are true. Just because you think it, doesn't make it true.

Third, change your thoughts based on the truth of God's Word. Consider if your thoughts line up with what God's Word says is true. If not, the next time you think this same thought, challenge yourself to believe what is true instead.

Reflection: In what areas of life do you need to take your thoughts captive to obey Christ?

Day 23 devotion video: https://youtu.be/RFujGTeLfp0

Day 24: How to Know When to Speak and When to Be Silent

Bible passage:

The Lord will fight for you, and you have only to be silent.

Exodus 14:14

Today's Bible verse gives you a wonderful reminder that sometimes you don't need to speak because God will defend you. The context of the verse is Moses reminding the Israelites of this after they escaped from Egypt where they had been slaves. Now, they are about to cross the Red Sea and God will protect them from harm.

I find great comfort in this passage, but it also challenges me. In other parts of Scripture God commands people to speak. In fact, earlier in this same story God told Moses to go to Pharaoh and command that he let the Israelite people go. That's the opposite of staying silent!

How do you know when to speak and when to stay silent? Use the concept of Scripture interpreting Scripture to find the answer. Here are three questions to ask yourself during times that you are unsure if you should speak or stay silent.

1. **Who or what am I defending?** If you are defending yourself, it may be best to stay silent and allow God to defend you. If you are defending God,

question your motives. While it is important to speak the truth about who God is, God does not need you to defend him. Sharing your personal testimony of faith is the way to win others for Christ. If you are defending those who cannot defend themselves, speaking up may be your calling.

2. **Who or what am I glorifying?** If speaking up will bring glory to God, this is motivated from a pure heart. If you are defending your own pride, it's best to stay silent.

3. **Who or what am I trusting?** Are you speaking out by trusting in your own words to prove your position? During these times, it may be better to stay quiet. Trust in God to take care of your needs instead.

By using these questions as a guide, you will be able to discern whether you should speak out or stay silent.

Reflection question: Think of a time you spoke up when it would have better to be silent, and a time when you were silent, but it would have been better to speak up. How can you use what you learned from these experiences?

Day 24 devotion video: https://youtu.be/5u6-PrCGgX8

Day 25: A Prayer for Peace

Bible passage:

Peace I leave with you; my peace I give to you. Not as the world gives do I give to you. Let not your hearts be troubled, neither let them be afraid.

John 14:27

God gives peace that goes beyond all human understanding. The world today needs peace with our government and citizens. You need peace in your relationships and with your own thoughts.

Let's pray together for peace. Take a few minutes to reflect on each area of your life as a prayer. Complete the sentence with ways you need God to bring peace into the world and your life.

Lord God, thank you for the peace you give us that passes all understanding.

We pray for peace today, Lord.

We pray for peace in our world…

We pray for peace in our relationships…

We pray for peace in our marriages…

We pray for peace with our work…

We pray for peace in ourselves…

In Jesus' name we pray. Amen.

Reflection question: In what areas of life do you especially need God's peace today?

Day 25 devotion video: https://youtu.be/hV1wc5o0kVw

Day 26: Struck Down but Not Destroyed

Bible Passage:

But we have this treasure in jars of clay, to show that the surpassing power belongs to God and not to us. We are afflicted in every way, but not crushed; perplexed, but not driven to despair; persecuted, but not forsaken; struck down, but not destroyed.

2 Corinthians 4:7-9

In today's busy world, overwhelm comes often. Home and work situations, challenging relationships, and troubling economic and government situations press in.

This Bible passage is a reminder that you are not crushed by the stress of it all. You have the Father your Creator, the Son your Savior, and the Holy Spirit your Comforter. Father, Son, and Holy Spirit go with you, live in you, and guide you.

You might be hard pressed, but you won't be crushed.

Perhaps you are perplexed, but there's no need to be dismayed.

People may persecute you, but you are not abandoned. God is with you and in you.

The world might strike you down, but you will not be destroyed.

Reflection question: In what ways are you feeling overwhelmed or struck down? How does today's Bible verse give you hope?

Day 26 devotion video: https://youtu.be/P7DNqEUHlTc

Day 27: How Big Are Your Problems?

Bible passage:

So we do not lose heart. Though our outer self is wasting away, our inner self is being renewed day by day. For this light momentary affliction is preparing for us an eternal weight of glory beyond all comparison, as we look not to the things that are seen but to the things that are unseen. For the things that are seen are transient, but the things that are unseen are eternal.

2 Corinthians 4:16-18

When you are in the middle of a problem, doesn't it feel gigantic? The problem may seem time-consuming, heart-consuming, and simply overwhelming.

Remember that compared to the course of a lifetime and on into eternity, this moment will be a small speck. In fact, it will be microscopic! Second Corinthians chapter four says that your current problems are light afflictions. This isn't to say your problems aren't real or your feelings aren't legitimate. Instead, God's Word is giving you a reminder that compared to eternity, today's problems will be insignificant.

Reflection question: In what ways do today's problems seem huge? How does looking at them considering eternity make a difference?

Day 27 devotion video: - https://youtu.be/-kZiPzfp_fl

Day 28: How to See with Eyes of Faith

Bible passage:

So we have come to know and to believe the love that God has for us. God is love, and whoever abides in love abides in God, and God abides in him. By this is love perfected with us, so that we may have confidence for the day of judgment, because as he is so also are we in this world. There is no fear in love, but perfect love casts out fear. For fear has to do with punishment, and whoever fears has not been perfected in love. We love because he first loved us.

1 John 4:16-19

During our toughest years of parenting our son with mental health issues, I decided that no matter how difficult his behaviors, I would look at him with eyes of faith. No matter how things looked on the outside, I chose to love him with God's love.

This was incredibly difficult to do because his behaviors included attacking me, hurting other children, destroying property, and telling me every day that he hated me. I was beaten down emotionally, scared, and exhausted. Yet, I chose to keep a kernel of hope and faith inside me that my son would succeed. This was looking at him with eyes of faith.

Keep in mind that looking at someone with eyes of faith is not blind optimism, and it's not the same as trust. Trust must be earned. Loving someone with God's love is unconditional.

God may be calling you to love someone with eyes of faith. Will you answer the call?

Reflection question: Who do you need to see with eyes of faith today?

Day 28 devotion video: https://youtu.be/RiTmPr47FP4

Day 29: How to Trust What You Cannot See

Bible passage:

If indeed by putting it on we may not be found naked. For while we are still in this tent, we groan, being burdened—not that we would be unclothed, but that we would be further clothed, so that what is mortal may be swallowed up by life. He who has prepared us for this very thing is God, who has given us the Spirit as a guarantee.

So we are always of good courage. We know that while we are at home in the body we are away from the Lord, for we walk by faith, not by sight.

2 Corinthians 5:3-7

The Bible tells us to walk by faith, not by sight, but how can we do this? How can we trust when we do not know for sure if it will happen in this lifetime?

During my one-hundred-pound weight loss journey, I learned to walk by faith. I kept thinking that if only I knew the result would happen, I could relax and be patient. I didn't know if I'd be able to lose one hundred pounds and keep it off. After all, I had tried many times and had not yet been successful.

I chose to trust that it was possible and believe it would happen. I knew God would never want me to stay stuck in overeating, compulsive food obsession, and binging. I trusted God for healing even when I had no evidence to prove it would happen.

This, my friend, is faith.

Reflection question: In what area of life do you need to walk by faith even though you cannot see evidence that it will happen?

Day 29 devotion video: https://youtu.be/ULYPfsuqtsc

Day 30: You Have This Light

Bible passage:

You are the light of the world. A city set on a hill cannot be hidden. Nor do people light a lamp and put it under a basket, but on a stand, and it gives light to all in the house. In the same way, let your light shine before others, so that they may see your good works and give glory to your Father who is in heaven.

Matthew 5:14-16

Do you struggle to accept compliments?

A few years ago, a friend gave me an incredible compliment. "You have this light," she said. "Other people are drawn to it. They want to be around you and they want to be like you." I was humbled by her kind words. As much as it has been my reaction to downplay a compliment, this time I didn't.

Instead, I took her words, and I stepped into them. I saw that she was right. People are drawn to me. I recognized areas of my life where this is true.

Upon further reflection, I came to see it wasn't that people are drawn to me, Sara. It's not my personality, leadership, or sense of humor. People are drawn to the light of Jesus they see at work in me.

You, my friend, have this same light. When you allow Jesus to shine through you, you have influence. People are drawn to you and want to be around you because they see Jesus in you. You are a light shining in this dark world.

People will be drawn to Christ because of your witness.

Reflection question: How can you allow the light of Christ to shine in you today?

Day 30 devotion video: https://youtu.be/XurN_iui4ZU

Conclusion

Thank you for joining me during the last thirty days as we have explored how your faith can be bigger than your fear.

Take some time today to reflect on these questions and if possible, write about them in your journal.

Reflection questions:

- What did you learn during this study about God and who He is?

- What did you learn about yourself?

- Which Bible passages were especially meaningful to you?

- In what ways will you be different after this study?

Say a prayer today thanking God for the ways He has grown you during the last thirty days.

Resources

Free *Fear Less* Bonus Pack: www.theholymess.com/fearless

Bible Reading Plan Notebook: www.theholymess.com/30-day-bible-reading-plan-notebook/

Sara's one-hundred-pound weight loss story: www.theholymess.com/100-lb-weight-loss-how-did-you-do-it/

Faithful Finish Lines Christian weight loss program: www.faithfulfinishlines.com

Parenting children with mental health issues: www.theholymess.com/standing/

Facebook: www.facebook.com/saraborgstede

Instagram: https://www.instagram.com/the_holy_mess_